10/05

The Primary Source Library of Famous Composers™

Wolfgang Amadeus
Mozart

Eric Michael Summerer

The Rosen Publishing Group's
PowerKids Press™
PRIMARY SOURCE

New York

To Stefanie

Published in 2006 by The Rosen Publishing Group, Inc.
29 East 21st Street, New York, NY 10010

First Edition

Editor: Frances E. Ruffin
Book Design: Michael J. Caroleo

Eric "Michaels" Summerer is music director and "morning guy" at the Internet radio station Beethoven.com.

Photo Credits: Cover (Mozart) Sammlung Alter Musikinstrumente, Vienna, Austria/Bridgeman Art Library; cover and interior borders (sheet music) Library of Congress, Music Division; p. 4 Glinka Museum of Music Culture, Moscow, Russia/Bridgeman Art Library; p. 7 Mozart Museum, Salzburg, Austria/Bridgeman Art Library; p. 8 The Art Archive/Society of the Friends of Music Vienna/Dagli Orti (A); p. 11 Haags Gemeentemuseum, Netherlands/Bridgeman Art Library; p. 12 (left) © Giraudon/Art Resource, NY, pp. 12 (right), 15 (right) © Scala/Art Resource, NY; pp. 14–15 Topkapi Palace Museum, Istanbul, Turkey/Bridgeman Art Library; p. 16 (top) Hulton/Archive/Getty Images; pp. 16 (bottom), 19 (bottom left, right), 20 (top) © Erich Lessing/Art Resource, NY; p. 19 (top left) Mozart Museum, Salzburg, Austria/Bridgeman Art Library; p. 20 (bottom) The Art Archive/Museum der Stadt Wien/Dagli Orti; p. 23 (top) © Superstock; p. 23 (bottom) Deutsches Theatermuseum, Munich, Germany/Roger-Viollet, Paris/Bridgeman Art Library; p. 24 (top left) The Art Archive/Biblioteca Nazionale Marciana Venice/Dagli Orti (A); p. 24 (top right) The Art Archive/Miramare Palace Trieste/Dagli Orti (A); p. 24 (bottom) Historisches Museum der Stadt, Vienna, Austria/Bridgeman Art Library; p. 27 (top) © Austrian Archives/Corbis; p. 27 (bottom) The Art Archive/Museo Teatrale alla Scala Milan/Dagli Orti (A).

Library of Congress Cataloging-in-Publication Data

Summerer, Eric Michael.
Wolfgang Amadeus Mozart / Eric Michael Summerer.
  p. cm. — (Primary source library of famous composers)
Summary: Introduces Wolfgang Amadeus Mozart, one of the best-known and busiest composers of all time who, as a child, played for royalty but later tried to break away from those who offered steady work but treated him badly.
Includes bibliographical references (p.   ) and index.
ISBN 1-4042-2772-5 (lib. bdg.)
1. Mozart, Wolfgang Amadeus, 1756–1791—Juvenile literature. 2. Composers—Austria—Biography—Juvenile literature. [1. Mozart, Wolfgang Amadeus, 1756–1791. 2. Composers.] I. Title. II. Series.
ML3930.M9 S84 2005
780.92—dc22

2003015452

Manufactured in the United States of America

Contents

A Busy Composer

Wolfgang Amadeus Mozart was one of the busiest and most productive **composers** of all time. He lived for only 35 years. During that time, he wrote more than 600 different musical **compositions**. As a child he toured Europe, and he **performed** for royalty. All were surprised that such a young boy could be such a talented **musician**. He was so well liked that some called him the most-kissed little boy in Europe. As he grew older, Mozart tried to break away from the **aristocrats** who hired musicians and paid them for the music that they created. They offered him a steady job, but they also treated him and other musicians with very little respect. Without their support, Mozart never made enough money to be successful. Nevertheless, he became such a respected musician and composer that he made it possible for composers to be treated as artists.

This is a painting of Wolfgang Amadeus Mozart as a young man wearing a white, powdered wig.

Beloved of God

Mozart was born on January 27, 1756, in Salzburg. Salzburg was a **city-state** between Austria and Bavaria, in the area that is now called Germany. Mozart was so small and weak when he was born that his father, Leopold, called his birth a **miracle**. His full name was Joannes Chrysostomus Wolfgangus Theophilus Mozart, but he liked to call himself Wolfgang Amadeus for short. "Theophilus" and "Amadeus" both mean **"beloved** of God." Wolfgang's older sister, Maria Anna, also had a shortened name, Nannerl. Their father, Leopold, was the kapellmeister, or music director, for the Prince of Salzburg. Leopold wrote a famous paper about how to play the **violin**. Their mother, Anna Maria, was a pleasant housewife who loved her children very much.

Wolfgang's father was proud of his children's musical abilities. Wolfgang and Nannerl were children when they sat for this oil painting.

Nannerl started piano lessons at age seven. At age three, Wolfgang started to learn the same music that his sister played. By the age of five, he was composing short pieces of his own music. Leopold realized that his son was a musical **prodigy**, which means he was a talented musician at a very young age. People in Europe enjoyed seeing musical prodigies perform during the eighteenth century. They were as popular as pop music stars are today. Leopold felt that it was his duty to **nurture** his son's talent, so he took Nannerl and Wolfgang on a tour of different cities when Wolfgang was only six. The Mozart children played in palaces all over Europe.

Wolfgang did not go to school, because he spent all of his time traveling and playing music. His father taught Wolfgang his lessons. Wolfgang loved math, and he learned to speak 15 languages.

This is an image of Mozart composing music. During Mozart's tour of Europe, everyone enjoyed seeing the little boy play such beautiful music.

In addition to playing the piano in the **traditional** manner, Wolfgang pleased **audiences** by performing musical tricks. He played the **keyboard** with the keys covered by a cloth. He often improvised during a **concert**, which means he composed a new piece of music as he was playing it. Wolfgang also had an ability called perfect pitch, which means he could name a musical note just by hearing it played.

Mozart could look at a sheet of music and play it perfectly the first time. While visiting Rome, Italy, Wolfgang visited the Sistine Chapel at the **Vatican** to hear the "Miserere," a choral piece based on the Catholic **Mass.** Having heard it only once, Mozart was able to write down the notes of the music without a mistake.

The Mozart family, shown here, performed in many cities. The father, Leopold, played the violin, Nannerl sang, and Wolfgang played the piano.

Mozart hated the trumpet and the flute. As an adult, people paid him to write music for the flute, but he did not enjoy it. Wolfgang's ears were so sensitive that any loud noise made him sick.

When the great composer Franz Joseph Haydn met Wolfgang, he told Leopold, "Before God, and as an honest man, I tell you that your son is the greatest composer known to me."

In Paris, France, Wolfgang met Marie-Antoinette. When young Wolfgang asked her to marry him, she turned him down. They were both seven years old at the time. Later she became queen of France, from 1774 to 1793. While in Paris, Wolfgang **published** four **piano sonatas.** Everyone who heard them was surprised that a child had written them. In 1764, the Mozarts traveled to London. There Wolfgang studied with Johann Christian Bach, known as J. C. Bach, the youngest son of composer Johann Sebastian Bach. J. C. Bach taught Wolfgang a lot about writing **symphonies.** Mozart wrote his first three symphonies while living in England. The family stopped its tour when Wolfgang came down with **smallpox** when he was 11.

Mozart loved the color red. He had five red coats and a white coat for performing in court. Inset: Marie-Antoinette is shown as an adult.

Opera is a kind of musical theater that was first performed in Italy in the seventeenth century. In an opera, performers tell a story completely through singing. The first operas were written in Italian. Since then, operas have been written in German, French, English, and many other languages. In Mozart's time, people considered opera to be the finest form of musical art.

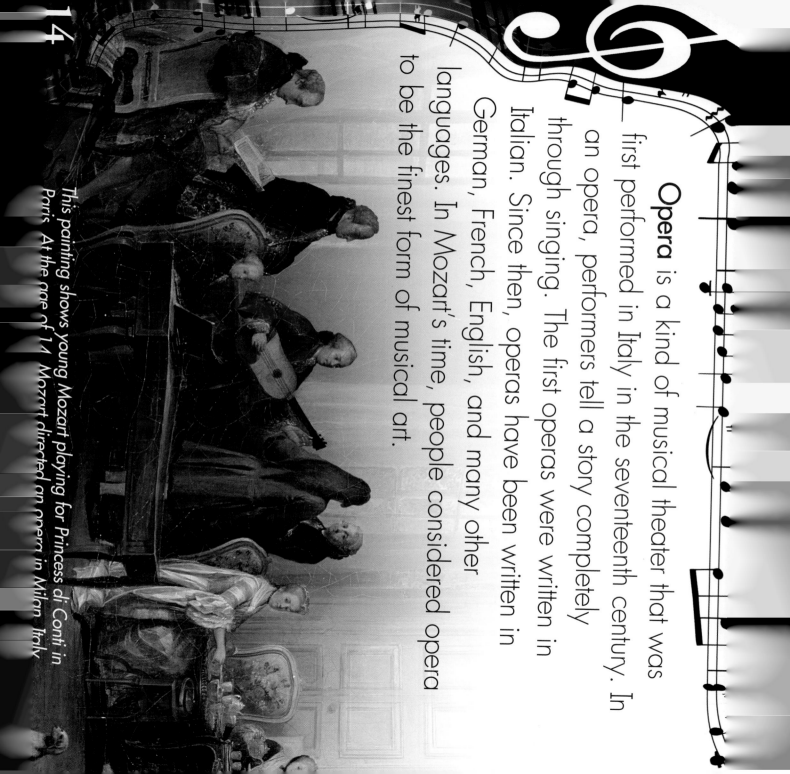

This painting shows young Mozart playing for Princess di Conti in Paris. At the age of 14, Mozart directed an opera in Milan, Italy.

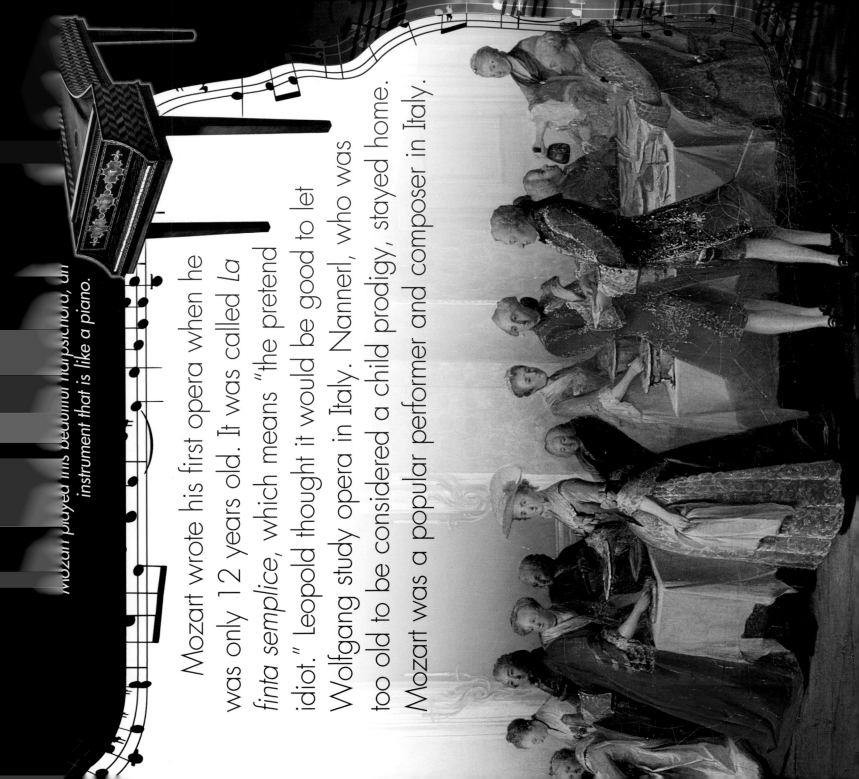

Mozart played his beautiful harpsichord, an instrument that is like a piano.

Mozart wrote his first opera when he was only 12 years old. It was called *La finta semplice*, which means "the pretend idiot." Leopold thought it would be good to let Wolfgang study opera in Italy. Nannerl, who was too old to be considered a child prodigy, stayed home. Mozart was a popular performer and composer in Italy.

Hieronymus Josef Graf von Colloredo (1732–1812) became the Prince Archbishop of Salzburg, Austria. He kept Wolfgang Mozart as his concertmaster. However, he made life difficult for Mozart, and he fired the composer in 1781.

A Cruel Boss

During Mozart's time, the best job for a musician was to work for an aristocrat who owned his or her own **orchestra**. These musicians, however, were treated no better than cooks and servants. The Prince of Salzburg was kind enough to give Wolfgang a job in **court** while letting him travel and perform with other orchestras. When the prince died in 1771, Wolfgang's new boss was Count Hieronymus Colloredo, who was **cruel** to Mozart. He forced Mozart to follow him to far-off cities and rarely let Mozart perform anywhere without his permission. Wolfgang could not earn enough money to live comfortably, because he was unable to perform his own concerts. In 1781, he got so angry that he started to yell at the count. Mozart was fired and kicked out the door of the count's palace and down his front stairs.

This is the palace where Count Colloredo kicked Mozart down the stairs.
Inset: This is a painting of Count Colloredo.

Mozart in Love

While traveling through Mannheim, Germany, in 1777, Mozart met and fell in love with a young opera singer named Aloysia Weber. He was 21 years old at the time. Mozart's father reminded him that he was traveling to find a job, not to fall in love. Aloysia lost interest in him, but she had a sister named Constanze who lived in Vienna. When Mozart traveled to Vienna in 1781, he met and fell in love with Constanze. They were married the following year. Mozart's father was unhappy with the marriage. Constanze came from a poor family. He worried that Wolfgang would not be able to **support** himself and his new bride.

Mozart and Constanze found a house in Vienna where he wrote music. Mozart and Constanze were in love, and they wanted to share their lives no matter how hard that might be.

These paintings show Mozart's wife Constanze (inset) and his sons, Carl Thomas and Franz Xavier (left). Mozart lived in this house (right) in Vienna with his family. It is where he wrote The Marriage of Figaro.

Mozart never seemed to have enough money. One reason was that when he played for royalty they paid him with gifts, such as watches or **snuffboxes**, instead of money. Without steady work in a court orchestra, Mozart also had to depend on whatever money that his operas and other compositions could bring in when they were performed by singers and orchestras. To make matters worse, Mozart spent more money than he earned. He gave huge parties and lived in large, **expensive** apartments. In fact, the Mozarts often had to move because they could not pay the rent. Some orchestras paid him to make new **arrangements** of other composers' music. Mozart got help when he joined a secret club and became a Freemason.

Mozart cared a great deal about his appearance. He often dressed in a velvet coat and wore a little gold sword. He even wore an apron when he wrote music so that he would not get ink on his clothes.

Rich members of Mozart's club gave him money. Here he is being presented to the club. Inset: These are a few of Mozart's snuffboxes.

In 1785, Mozart started to write his most famous opera, The Marriage of Figaro. The story is about a servant named Figaro and his wish to marry the beautiful Susanna. To marry, they have to fool their boss, the count, who has lost interest in his own wife. He finds Susanna pretty. At the end of the opera, Susanna and the countess switch clothes, and the count swears his love for the countess, whom he thinks is Susanna. When the countess tells the count who she really is, he asks her to forgive him. She does and they all live happily ever after. Audiences loved The Marriage of Figaro when it was first performed in Vienna in 1786. It was even more popular with audiences in Prague, in what is now the Czech Republic. People loved to sing songs from the opera. The following year Mozart wrote another much-loved opera, Don Giovanni.

This painting is a scene from Mozart's opera The Marriage of Figaro. Inset: This is a 1786 ad for The Marriage of Figaro at a theater in Vienna.

During the summer of 1788, Mozart wrote his final three symphonies, as well as other pieces, during a period of only three months.

The last few years of Mozart's life were very **difficult** ones for him. In 1790, Emperor Joseph II asked Mozart to write an opera. Mozart wrote an opera called *Cosi fan tutte*, which means "they are all the same." The opera was a huge hit, but the emperor died less than a month after it opened and Mozart lost money. He also lost money later that year when a German opera company called off performing his opera *Don Giovanni*.

However, Mozart enjoyed a few happy moments during this time. He completed his **Clarinet Concerto** in A Major and one of the most popular operas of all time, *The Magic Flute*. Mozart still had no steady job. He overworked in his struggle to earn a living and was destroying his own health.

Bottom: *This is a scene from Mozart's opera* The Magic Flute. *Top Right: Joseph II is shown in this painting. At the top is Music from* Cosi fan tutte.

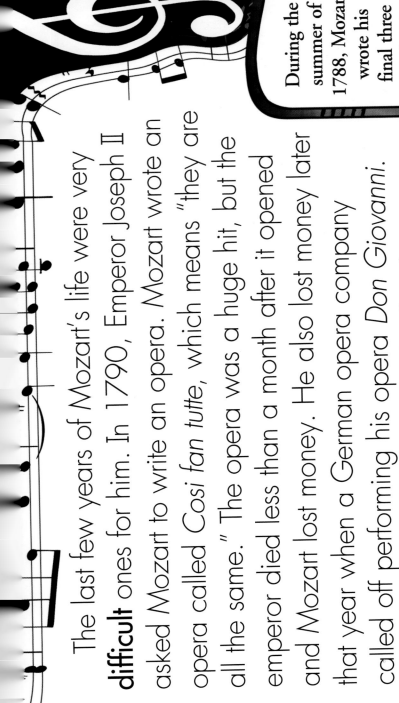

In July 1791, a man dressed in gray visited Mozart and asked him to write a requiem, which is a piece of music written to honor the dead. The request came from Count Franz Walsegg-Stuppach. He was a nobleman who often asked great composers to write music that he later claimed to have written himself. Mozart became very **paranoid**. He wrote the piece though he was sure that he was writing the requiem for his own **funeral**. Mozart never finished Requiem. On December 4, he gathered his friends and family around him. He asked them to sing "Lacrymosa," which means tearful, with him. If was the last song that he had completed for his Requiem. Crying, he said good-bye to his guests around midnight. By 1:00 A.M., Mozart was dead. He was 35. The Mozarts had very little money. His wife could only give him a simple funeral.

A painting shows Mozart's simple and lonely funeral. Inset: The sheet music at the top of the page is "Lacrymosa" from Mozart's Requiem.

Mozart Lives On

Wolfgang Amadeus Mozart died more than 200 years ago, but his music is still popular today. His operas, especially The Marriage of Figaro, The Magic Flute, and Don Giovanni, are performed by opera companies around the world.

In 1987, an original **manuscript** containing nine of his symphonies sold for $4.34 million.

Amadeus, a 1984 Hollywood film about Mozart's life, featured many of his compositions. His music can be heard in television productions and in many movies, including JFK and Philadelphia. Elvira Madigan, a 1967 movie, used his Piano Concerto No. 21.

Mozart wrote so much music people love that they may hear his work when they least expect it.

Listening to Mozart

Mozart wrote more than 600 musical compositions, including 25 piano concertos, 27 string quartets, 21 Masses, and 56 symphonies. Here are some of Mozart's works that you might enjoy.

Requiem

This is Mozart's final piece. He wasn't able to finish it before he died.

Eine kleine Nachtmusik

This is a very famous composition. Its name means "a little night music."

The Marriage of Figaro

This is Mozart's most popular opera.

Piano Concerto No. 21

This music was used in the film *Elvira Madigan.*

Timeline

1756 Wolfgang Amadeus Mozart is born in Salzburg, Austria.
1759 Mozart starts to play the piano at age three.
1762 Wolfgang and sister Nannerl tour Europe.
1767 Mozart writes his first opera at age 12.
1782 Mozart marries Constanze Weber.
1784 Their first son, Carl Thomas, is born.
1786 Mozart writes *The Marriage of Figaro*, his most famous opera.
1788 Mozart writes his last three symphonies and eight other works in one summer.
1791 Mozart dies at the age of 35.

Musical Terms

arrangements (uh-RAYNJ-ments) Rewriting a piece of music using different instruments.

clarinet (kler-uh-NET) A musical instrument shaped like a tube that is blown into to make music.

composers (kom-POH-zerz) People who write music.

compositions (kom-puh-ZIH-shunz) Pieces of writing or music.

concert (KON-sert) A public musical performance.

concerto (kun-CHER-toh) Music created for an orchestra and one or more solo, or single, instruments.

keyboard (KEE-bord) An instrument that uses a set of keys, such as a piano or an organ.

manuscript (MAN-yuh-skript) An article, a book, or a sheet of music that is handwritten or typed.

Mass (MAS) Musical pieces based on church services.

musician (myoo-ZIH-shun) A person who writes, plays, or sings music.

opera (AH-pruh) A form of theater in which the story is told through singing.

orchestra (OR-kes-truh) A group of people who play music together.

performed (per-FORMD) To have sung, danced, acted, or played an instrument.

piano (pee-A-noh) A keyboard instrument with small hammers that strike wire strings to make music.

sonatas (suh-NAH-tuz) Compositions for one to four instruments, one of which is usually a keyboard.

symphonies (SIM-fuh-neez) Long musical compositions written for an orchestra.

violin (vy-uh-LIN) A small instrument that makes sound when a bow is drawn over its strings.

Glossary

aristocrats (uh-RIS-tuh-krats) Members of the wealthy upper class.

audiences (AH-dee-ints-ez) Groups of people who watch or listen to something.

beloved (bih-LUVD) Dearly loved.

city-state (SIH-tee-stayt) An independent state made up of a city and its surrounding areas.

court (KORT) The king, queen, or other ruler's advisers and officers.

cruel (KROOL) Causing pain or suffering.

difficult (DIH-fih-kult) Hard to do or understand.

expensive (ek-SPEN-siv) Costing a lot of money.

funeral (FYOON-rul) The service held when burying the dead.

miracle (MEER-uh-kul) A wonderful or an unusual event said to have been done by God.

nurture (NUR-chur) To help to grow.

paranoid (PER-uh-noyd) To be very fearful and mistrustful.

prodigy (PRAH-deh-jee) A child who is very smart and talented in some way.

published (PUH-blishd) Printed so that people can read it.

smallpox (SMOL-poks) A serious sickness that causes a rash and leaves marks on the skin.

snuffboxes (SNUF-boks-ez) Containers for finely ground tobacco.

support (suh-PORT) To provide for by giving money or necessities.

traditional (truh-DIH-shuh-nul) Done in a way that has been passed down over time.

Vatican (VA-tih-ken) In Rome, the headquarters of the Pope, who is the head of the Roman Catholic Church.

Index

Primary Sources

Cover. This portrait of Mozart was painted by Barbara Krafft (1764–1825).

Page 4. An oil-on-canvas painting by Giuseppe or Josef Grassi (1759–1791). It is part of the Glinka Museum of Culture, Moscow, Russia.

Page 7. The miniature-on-ivory portrait of Mozart and his sister, Nannerl, was painted by Eusebius Johann Alphen (1751–1829).

Page 8. The Young Wolfgang Amadeus Mozart is a nineteenth-century engraving at the Society of the Friends of Music, Vienna, Austria.

Page 11. An engraving by Louis Carrogis Carmontelle (1717–1806) shows Leopold Mozart and his children, Nannerl and Wolfgang.

Page 12. Inset. This oil-on-canvas portrait of Marie-Antoinette of Austria is held at Chateaux de Versailles et de Trianon, Versailles, France.

Page 14. Inset. Mozart gives a concert for Princess di Conti in English Tea, an oil-on-canvas painting by Michel Barthelemy Ollivier (1712–1784).

Page 14. Mozart composed the opera Mitridate Re diPonto on this harpsichord, which was created by Antonio Scotti in 1753.

Page 16. This engraving by Salomon Kleiner (1700–1761) shows the House of the Order of Teutonic Knights in Vienna, Austria.

Page 19. Bottom Left. This is a portrait of Carl and Wolfgang Mozart, children of Wolfgang Amadeus and Constanze Mozart, at ages 13 and 16. It was painted by Hans Hansen (1769–1829).

Page 19. The watercolor painting of this house on Schulerstrasse in Vienna, where Mozart composed The Marriage of Figaro, was made by H. Janda circa 1900.

Page 20. Meeting of Vienna Masonic Lodge Where Wolfgang Amadeus Mozart Was Present was created in 1790. It is located at the Museum der Stadt Wien.

Page 24. Act II from The Magic Flute, engraving, Joseph & Peter Schaffer (1780–1810).

Web Sites

Due to the changing nature of Internet links, PowerKids Press has developed an online list of Web Sites related to the subject of this book. This site is updated regularly. Please use this link to access the list:

www.powerkidslinks.com/plfc/mozart/